JEANNETTE RANKIN

To young Jeannettes everywhere
—T. M.

For Sharon
—D. A.

Thank-yous: The Montana State Historical Society, Helena, MT, with special thanks to Dave Walters and Jodie Foley

The Arthur and Elizabeth Schlesinger Library on the History of Women in America, Radcliffe College, Cambridge, MA

The Jeannette Rankin Foundation, Athens, GA

Margaret K. McElderry Books · An imprint of Simon & Schuster Children's Publishing Division · 1230 Avenue of the Americas, New York, New York 10020 · Text copyright © 2006 by Trish Marx · Illustrations copyright © 2006 by Dan Andreasen · All rights reserved, including the right of reproduction in whole or in part in any form. · Book design by Polly Kanevsky and Abelardo Martínez · The text for this book is set in Daily News. · The illustrations for this book are rendered in graphite drawings and oil paintings on gessoed illustration board. · Manufactured in China · 10 9 8 7 6 5 4 3 2 1 · Library of Congress Cataloging-in-Publication Data · Marx, Trish. · Jeannette Rankin : First Lady of Congress / Trish Marx ; illustrated by Dan Andreasen.—1st ed. · p. cm. · ISBN-13: 978-0-689-86290-8 · ISBN-10: 0-689-86290-3 (hardcover) · 1. Rankin, Jeannette, 1880–1973—Juvenile literature. 2. Legislators—United States—Biography—Juvenile literature. 3. United States. Congress. House—Biography—Juvenile literature. I. Title. · E748.R223M37 2006 · 328.73'092—dc22 · 2004004141

FIRST EDITION

JEANNETTE RANKIN
First Lady of Congress

~

Trish Marx
Illustrated by Dan Andreasen

Margaret K. McElderry Books
New York London Toronto Sydney

Chapter One
BIG SKY COUNTRY
1880–1892

———— ❧ ————

Jeannette Rankin was born in Montana—
Big Sky Country.
The sky was as blue as the feathers on a blue jay's back,
the trees were tall, and the mountains were high.
Out in Big Sky Country, people were used to big.
Big ideas, big promises, big plans.
That's what it took to survive.
And there was nobody out there to tell them any different.

Jeannette's father, John, had traveled to Montana Territory
from Canada in 1869, looking for gold and adventure
and opportunities.
He had come by boat, traveling the Missouri River
until he ran aground on a sandbar.
Heaving his tool chest onto his back, John walked to
the nearest town, Fort Benton.
Instead of gold, he found trees.
He built a sawmill there, and when other people
started coming to Montana Territory,
big, gruff, smart John sold them pine boards
for houses and for schools and for wooden sidewalks
to cover the muddy paths in town—
and make it a town proper.

Jeannette's mother, Olive Pickering, came from New Hampshire
with her sister Mandana in 1878.
Olive was shy around people yet not shy about adventure.
Mandana returned back east, but Olive stayed to teach
in a one-room schoolhouse.
When Olive met John Rankin, she saw in him her intellectual match.
She was willing to let him be the outspoken one,
knowing that she was his center.

John and Olive married and started a family.
Jeannette was born first—on June 11, 1880.
Next came Philena, who died in childhood, then Harriet, Mary,
Wellington, Grace, and Edna.

Montana Territory became a state in 1889.
There was a lot to do in this new land,
though not many people to do it.
Every person had to work hard.
Every person was important,
even nine-year-old Jeannette.

Living all summer on a ranch outside the town of Missoula,
the Rankins had to do most things for themselves.
There were berries to pick and cows to milk, trees to cut
and horses to tame, ranch hands to feed,
stitching and sewing and always the little ones to watch.
For fun on hot summer days, Jeannette and her brother,
Wellington, would run to the mill pond and play on the logs,
slipping into the cool water again and again.

One day when Jeannette was twelve,
she was helping out with the chores.
Suddenly the frightened neighing of a horse split the quiet of the afternoon.
Jeannette ran to the corral.
A sturdy cow horse had a bloody gash on his shoulder.
The skin was hanging down.

"Throw the horse," she called to the ranch hands.
She ran into the house and came out with her mother's sewing kit.
With the biggest needle and the strongest thread,
Jeannette stitched up the wound and bound it with strips of cloth.

When Jeannette's father got home, he said, "Good work, Jeannette."
Jeannette was pleased, but she had just done her job
keeping the place up and running,
as women did all over Montana.

Chapter Two
GO! GO! GO . . .
AT THE FIRST OPPORTUNITY, GO!*
1898–1909

John and Olive wanted all of their children to be educated,
even though at that time many women did not finish high school
and very few went to college.
John helped to open a new school in Missoula—the University of Montana.
Jeannette was the first Rankin child to attend the university.
She studied seashells because she liked the biology professor.
But she didn't know what she really wanted to do with her life.
After graduation she taught in small country schools.
Wellington went out east to attend Harvard, a school for boys in
Cambridge, outside of Boston, Massachusetts.
"Come and visit," he wrote to Jeannette.

The trip from Montana to Massachusetts was a long journey—
three thousand miles—for a woman to make.
But Jeannette persuaded a friend from college to join her,
and they had a grand adventure!

*Taken from a journal Jeannette kept in college

When Jeannette and her friend arrived in Boston, Wellington took them to parties and lectures. He arranged for teas and shopping trips. Wellington even brought them down to Washington, D.C., for President Theodore Roosevelt's inaugural ball.
Jeannette piled her dark hair high on her head and wore a stylish dress for the ball. She danced all night and met many young men.

But Jeannette wanted something more.
In Boston she had glimpsed crowded, dirty streets
and children in rags, begging for money.
She wanted to get a closer look at these people and places.
"Take me to the slums," she said to Wellington.
"I want to see how the people live there."

Wellington knew that if he didn't take Jeannette, she would find a way to get to the slums on her own, so he arranged for a tour.
As they rode past cramped, airless buildings filled with children who had no place to play, women hanging the wash out of their windows, and noise and dirt and sickness, Jeannette knew what she wanted to do.
More than going to the parties or teas or balls,
she wanted to help to make women's lives better.
Women had to work hard in Montana, but they got something for it—
they got fresh air and big, blue skies and good food,
and they got respect.
Maybe Jeannette could help *all* women to get better lives.
Maybe if women could vote in elections like men,
then women could vote for laws that would make their lives,
and the lives of their children, better.

Jeannette went back to Montana.
She worked in a settlement house, where mothers and children could live
if they didn't have a home.
She worked with orphaned children, placing them with families.
She worked in schools. She helped the people she met each day.
But this work wasn't reaching enough people.
What could she do that would help even more women and children
and families?

Once again, she packed her bags and rode the train east—this time
to New York City, where she studied social work at the New York
School of Philanthropy.
Some of her courses were in classrooms.
Others took her out to factories and slums.
Whenever she went to the night police court
with women she was helping,
she carried a police officer's
billy club in her velvet bag.

It was 1909, a progressive time when people were searching for ways
to help the poor to find a voice.
Jeannette was swept up in this reformist movement.
She moved back west to Washington State, where she worked in orphanages.
It was discouraging when children were returned back to the orphanage
after Jeannette had found a home for them.
The children had few rights and fewer protections.
Jeannette asked questions:
What would cause this situation to change?
Would it be one person helping another?
Or would it be one person causing a change that would reach many people?
And what would cause a change that big?

Laws, thought Jeannette. *I've been trying to help women to have better lives using
the laws we already have. But what if the laws are wrong or don't go far enough?*
Jeannette figured that if she could change some of the laws,
that would be something . . . and that might be enough.

Chapter Three
VOTES FOR WOMEN!
1910–1914

———— ❧ ————

Jeannette was almost thirty years old.
She was smart.
She was educated.
And she wanted to make a difference.

She enrolled at the University of Washington in Seattle,
where she could study about how to make and change laws.

One rainy evening she saw a stack of posters on a table:
ROOSEVELT FOR WOMEN'S VOTE.
Theodore Roosevelt, the president whose inaugural ball
she had danced at in Washington, D.C., supported the vote
for women!
The right to vote was called suffrage, and since only the men
of Washington State had suffrage, or could vote, they would be
the ones voting for, or against, women's suffrage.
Jeannette believed that the men needed to understand
how important suffrage was for women so they would vote for it
and it would become a law.
Then women would also be able to make decisions about how they
wanted to live.

Jeannette tramped up and down the streets of Seattle, tacking posters
to fences and doors and store windows.
She stopped at the barber shop. This was a place for men,
for men's jokes and men's talk, a place where women didn't go.
Jeannette took a deep breath and walked in.
The men stared.
Jeannette boldly stepped to the window and tacked up a poster for suffrage.
Then she turned to the men.
"Thank you," she said, smiling. "We'd appreciate your vote."

After this, was there anything Jeannette could not do?
If women could vote, they would make laws to change the cramped
settlement houses and orphanages.
If women could vote, they would vote for laws to give children safer food
and better schools.
If they could vote, women—who rose at dawn, cooked, ironed, scrubbed,
baked, swept, mended, and cooked again, yet who were listed on census
reports as "without occupation"—would be able to change their lives.

Jeannette worked alongside many other women fighting for suffrage.
They rented lecture halls and hired speakers.
Sometimes only fifteen people showed up to listen.
But when the election day came and the ballots were counted, the men
had voted for suffrage for women.
The women of Washington could vote!
Finally Jeannette was helping to change social problems through legislation.

Washington was only the fifth state in the nation to give women
the right to vote.
There were so many more states. . . .

VOTES FOR WOMEN

Jeannette went back to Montana for Christmas.

It was 1910, and a suffrage bill had been introduced into the Montana legislature.

The Equal Franchise Society asked Jeannette to speak for the bill in front of the legislature, where no woman had ever given a speech.

Jeannette had a month to prepare.

She practiced in front of Wellington, who was now home from Harvard.

The legislature got ready for Jeannette, too.

In the State Capitol building in Helena, where Jeannette was to speak, the legislators banned smoking. They removed the spittoons. They said that no one could swear. And they each donated fifty cents to buy Jeannette a huge bouquet of violets.

On the day of Jeannette's speech the galleries, where observers sat, were hot and crowded, and dotted with the bright gowns and feathered hats of the women who had come to cheer Jeannette on.

"I was born in Montana," Jeannette started.

There was thunderous applause.

Then she proposed equal pay for equal work and asked that women be able to vote for laws, such as milk inspections, that would help their children. The applause turned to laughter and then to jokes.

One senator said that only women who had six children should be allowed to vote. Another senator called Jeannette "one lone woman who, unluckily, has not been able to ensnare a man."

Finally a senator rose and talked about how hard his mother had worked for her family.

"A woman like that," he said, "ought to have the right to vote."

But that day there were not enough votes to pass the suffrage bill in Montana.

That would take three more years of hard work.

In 1914, during the final months of the second suffrage campaign, Jeannette traveled nine thousand miles back and forth across Montana to fight for the bill.

She led a parade in Helena, marching alongside suffragists as well as small boys with hatbands proclaiming I WANT MY MOTHER TO VOTE.

This time the bill passed.

The women of Montana could vote.

Chapter Four

A WOMAN'S PLACE IS IN THE HOME
1915–1916

———— ⌒⌒⌒ ————

It was 1915.
Jeannette was back in Montana after a trip to New Zealand,
a country halfway around the world.
She had traveled there by herself, with only a purseful of money,
to rest and to think about her future.
She had come back filled with the spirit of the women there—
strong women, women who upped and did,
women who weren't afraid to change their lives.
Sitting in her mother's parlor, Jeannette was surrounded by
young women, by mothers, even grandmothers.
They had supported Jeannette when she campaigned for suffrage.
They liked her ideas, new and fresh and bold.
And now they had gathered together to hear about Jeannette's new idea.

Jeannette told them that they were like the women she had met
in New Zealand.
"Those women could do things, and so can you," she said.
"You can help elect a woman to the Congress of the United States.
You can help elect me."

Never mind that there had never before been a woman in Congress.
Jeannette wanted women to have the right to vote, but campaigning
state by state would be slow and difficult.
What was needed was a change in the Constitution of the United States—
a change that would guarantee all women in America the right to vote.
And one of the best ways to pass that amendment would be to have a
woman in Congress.

Then Jeannette told the women she had another reason to run
for Congress.
"I want to run so women won't have to send their sons to war," she said.
Jeannette was worried because war was breaking out in Europe.
She believed a country had a right to defend itself if invaded, but she
didn't believe in sending American troops to fight on foreign soil.
The Constitution gave Congress the power to vote for or against entering
a war. Jeannette wanted the people of Montana to know where she stood
on the issues.
"I'm not running for Congress," she told the women. "I am running for
women's suffrage and against war."

Her friends were astounded.
"Could she be serious?" they asked.
"Keep your sister from making a fool of herself," Wellington's friends advised.
But Jeannette didn't listen. Wellington didn't either.
He put a big map on the wall of his office, where he ran his ranch.
"I'll manage your campaign," he said. "And you will get elected."

Jeannette was one of five candidates running for Congress.
There were two Democrats, two Socialists, and two Republicans,
but neither Republican was a strong leader.
Because of her suffrage work, Jeannette was respected as someone who
could get things done.
So she ran as a Republican for a seat in the House of Representatives,
carving out a platform to express her progressive beliefs, which were more
humanitarian than Republican or Democrat.
She wanted an eight-hour work day for women.
She wanted better care for children, especially orphans.
She wanted people to know more about how politicians stood on the issues.
And she wanted the vote for women.

Jeannette was a good campaigner, visiting factories, mines, lumber camps, and railroad yards all over Montana, knocking on farmhouse doors, and speaking on street corners.

When people said, "A woman's place is in the home," Jeannette replied, "The way to protect the home is to have a say in the government."

When people said, "Women have smaller brains and can never think," Jeannette replied, "Think about what I am saying"—meaning she was making good sense!

Some women said they didn't care what Jeannette stood for—they just wanted to show that men weren't as smart as they thought they were.

In Fort Benton a brass band played for Jeannette.

Her supporters sent out thousands of penny postcards saying "Dear friends . . . we're going to vote for Jeannette Rankin. Hope you will."

Jeannette's mother put down her knitting, and her sisters put down their babies and their schoolbooks, to campaign door-to-door for Jeannette.

After her last campaign speech Jeannette went to vote—and voted for herself. It would take several days for the ballots to be collected from all over the state and counted by hand.

Jeannette tried to be patient, but later that day she picked up the phone and called the *Daily Missoulian*.

Too embarrassed to ask about herself, she asked the newspaper reporter on the line if Woodrow Wilson, a Democrat who was running for president of the United States, had won.

"Yes, he did," said the reporter.

Then she asked if Jeannette Rankin had been elected to Congress.

"Oh, she lost," he said.

The next day, November 8, the newspaper headlines announced that Jeannette had lost.

Jeannette was about to concede the election to her opponent,
George Farr, when Wellington called.
"You are going to win!" he boomed.
Montana was a big state, and the ballots
had to come to Helena by oxen, by train,
by horseback, over mountain passes,
and on rough roads.
Wellington knew that the ballots that hadn't
arrived yet were from places he had marked
on his map as being supportive of Jeannette.
So she held on.

Two days later, on November 10, 1916, all of the
votes were counted.
Jeannette was the first woman elected to the Congress
of the United States!
Newspapers around the country printed articles about her.
The *New York Times* wondered if Jeannette carried a
six-shooter and trimmed her skirts with fur because she was
from the untamed West.

The *Kentucky Courier-Journal* praised her, however, and asked
the question: "Breathes there a man with a heart so brave
that he would want to become one of a . . . body made up
of 434 women *and himself*."

Jeannette didn't mind what any of the papers said.
She was going to Congress!
She headed east to Washington, D.C.
Most congressmen were Republicans, so they were called the majority
party, and the Democrats were the minority party.
Jeannette had a lot to learn about how people got things done in Congress.
It was time to start the most important work of her life.

Chapter Five

TROUBLE IN WASHINGTON

Jeannette Rankin was thirty-six years old and famous.
Reporters and photographers followed her all over the capital.
She received marriage proposals in the mail. One toothpaste company
offered her five thousand dollars for a picture of her teeth.
The *New York Times* wrote:

"Her maiden speeches will be known
for charm and grace of manner.
But who on earth will chaperone
the member from Montana?"

Jeannette was upset about all of the attention she was getting as the first
woman in Congress. She wanted people to write about her *ideas,*
not her looks or her teeth or her clothes.

She was elected to the Sixty-fifth Congress, which was scheduled to start
in December 1917.
Before then, everyone wanted to hear the new congresswoman.

Jeannette traveled around the country giving speeches, and she was paid
the huge sum of five hundred dollars per speech.
Her contract for the tour included a line stating that if she were to ever
vote against the United States' going to war, then she would be forced to
leave the tour.
Maybe, just maybe, America would not be called into the Great War
raging in Europe.
Then Jeannette could work for the everyday things women needed and
for national suffrage, and she would not have to face the war vote.

On April 2, 1917, Jeannette was honored at a breakfast given by suffragettes in Washington, D.C.

When Jeannette rose to speak, the women stood and clapped.

Around her, Jeannette saw strong women who were turning to her for leadership.

But most of these women felt that if Jeannette were to vote against going to war, the women's cause would be hurt because women would be seen as weak.

"I promise . . ." was all Jeannette could say.

Terrified at the responsibility she had taken on, she sat down and stared at the table. She was going to have to gather her strength.

Later that day a reporter from the *Washington Times* called to interview her. "I am in a pretty predicament," she told him. "I have so much to learn that I don't know what to say and what not to say. So I have decided not to say anything at all for the present. . . ."

She was dreading the vote on whether America should help England fight in the Great War.

An emergency session was called in Congress.

At noon that day, Jeannette went to the congressional chambers in the Capitol building.

She carried a bouquet of yellow and purple flowers.

The day was filled with speeches, discussions, and anxious whispers about the war vote.

Finally that evening President Wilson spoke to both houses of Congress. He asked the senators and representatives to vote to "make the world safe for democracy." This meant voting to go to war.

Jeannette would have to make the most difficult decision of her life.

Jeannette went to her office. People crowded
   around her. She read telegrams from Montana.
   She listened to her friends, her staff, and her
   supporters.
      Then she listened to Wellington, who had
      come to Washington, D.C., to help her
      get started in her new position.
      "Be patient," he said. "Vote a man's vote.
      You will not be re-elected if you vote 'no.'"
      The suffragettes said, "The suffrage movement
      will suffer if you say 'no.'"
   Friends told her, "So what if you vote for war?
   You have many other battles to fight."
But Jeannette remembered her campaign promise
to the people of Montana.
"I will do everything in my power to keep our
 country out of war and your sons safe at home,"
 she had said.
      She told Wellington she would wait until the last
      minute to vote, so that she could think about it
      until the end.

The decision about going to war came to a vote on April 7, 1917.
Jeannette had been in Congress only six days.
She took her place in the congressional chambers.
"Miss Rankin."
Jeannette's name was called so she could cast her vote, but she
remained silent.
One representative said, "Little woman, you cannot afford not to vote."
Jeannette knew that every representative's name was called twice to vote.
If she didn't speak the first time, she would have another chance later.
Jeannette waited.

It was three o'clock in the morning when her name was called again.
In a clear voice Jeannette said,
"I want to stand by my country, but I cannot vote for war.
I vote 'no.'"

The "yes" votes won.
America was going to war.
But after the vote, six other representatives told Jeannette that
they wished they had had the courage to vote against war.
Wellington walked Jeannette back to her apartment. "You know,
you are not going to be re-elected," he said.
"I'm not interested in that," Jeannette said. "All I am interested in
is what they will say fifty years from now."

Jeannette finished out her term and ran for Congress again.
This time she hoped to be a senator from Montana.
But just as Wellington had predicted, she lost the election.
Still, she said, "Never for one second could I face the idea
that I would send young men to be killed for no other reason
than to save my seat in Congress."

The suffrage bill was passed in January 1919.
"If I am remembered for no other act," Jeannette said,
"I want to be remembered as the only woman
who ever voted to give women the right to vote."

Chapter Six
THE QUIET YEARS
1919–1937

———— ⌘ ————

After Jeannette lost the Montana Senate seat, she settled on a farm
outside of Athens, Georgia.
"The attitude of the South is toward peace," Jeannette said.
Southern congressmen and the Southern press had criticized America's
entry into war.
Jeannette felt that the South questioned the morality of war as she did.

Jeannette wanted to live simply. She turned an old shed into a cookhouse.
It had a kerosene stove, tar paper walls, and no running water.
She washed dishes under a tree near the well,
surrounded by the fragrance of honeysuckle and wild plums.
At night she read by lanterns and candles and slept in a sleeping porch.
The main house had a large fireplace, where she and her many guests
sat and talked late into the night.
She added an upper floor for her guests.
The staircase was narrow. When Jeannette's mother came to visit,
her corset got stuck in the top opening of the staircase and she
had to be pried loose!

Jeannette organized the Sunshine Club for young children living near her. The first order of the club was fun.

Jeannette bought a bolt of white fabric. "We're going to make bathing suits," she said to the girls.

She looked at the girls' faces staring at the plain cloth.

"Out of that?" one girl whispered. "We'll look like flour sacks."

"Okay," said Jeannette. "We'll dye the cloth."

"Pink," a voice piped up.

After the girls swam, cooked, read, or played games,
Jeannette talked to them about peace and law and women's rights.

Jeannette invited boys to join the Sunshine Club too.
The boys arrived barefoot on mules, sometimes carrying
a watermelon.
Jeannette would put the watermelon down the well
so it would be icy cold when they'd eat it.
After the boys played ragtime music on a French
or Jew's harp, or worked on radio sets,
they would haul the watermelon up from the well
and hammer it open for chunks of the juicy treat.

Although no longer in politics, Jeannette was determined to continue working for peace.

She started the Georgia Peace Society, an action group for nonviolent solutions to the world's problems.

She gave speeches and raised money so that people could learn how to settle disputes peacefully.

Jeannette's first house burned to the ground in a kerosene fire, so she moved into a sharecropper's shanty on thirty-three wooded acres.

Another family also lived on the property—the Robinsons.

Wonder Robinson did the heavy chores, and his wife, Mattie, helped with the cleaning.

The Robinson children watched Jeannette clear the creepers from around her home. Creepers were plants that would grow and strangle trees—and they were also hiding places for poisonous snakes.

"Ain't you afraid of nothing?" the children asked.

It was 1937, and with talk of trouble and unrest in Germany because of new policies started by a man named Adolph Hitler, how could Jeannette be afraid of a snake?

She was worried about another war.

Chapter Seven

THE HUSBAND OF A PRESIDENT

1938–1940

———— ⚬✣⚬ ————

The world watched as Hitler came to power.
He stormed Europe, taking over countries with lightning speed.
He also declared war on the Jewish people.

Franklin Roosevelt, the president of the United States, said that
Hitler's actions would destroy civilization, and that peace-loving nations
needed to stop him.
Jeannette knew this meant that America would send boys to war to stop Hitler.
But Jeannette did not change her mind about war.
She believed that many people in America felt as she did, and she wanted
to be their voice before it was too late.

Jeannette was fifty-nine years old in 1939. Twenty-three years had passed
since her last election in 1916.
Time had only strengthened her resolve that sending boys to war
was wrong, and that wars were not the way to solve problems.
Should she run for Congress again?
Jeannette spoke to Wellington in Montana. He was now a wealthy rancher.
She needed his advice and financial support.
"Move back to Montana," his voice boomed over the telephone.
"I'll help you run for Congress."

Jeannette went back home, and in June 1940 she filed for a seat in the United States House of Representatives from the Western District of Montana.
She started her campaign by talking to children. She told them about a congressman who had come to speak to her school when she was a child. He had talked to the boys, only turning to the girls at the end to say, "Perhaps one day you will be the wife of a president of the United States." So when Jeannette visited schools, she said, "There are opportunities for girls now and opportunities for boys, too.
Someday one of you may be the husband of a president."

Once again, Jeannette campaigned.
She talked to people wherever she found them—in the fields, on street corners, in their kitchens.
She told them that the real enemies of the country were hunger, want, unemployment, and disease.
She ran against one other Republican and one Democrat.
Her slogan was: "Prepare to the limit for *defense* [in order to] keep our men out of Europe."
She said that if Montanans did not want peace, then she did not want to represent them.

On November 4, 1940, Jeannette was elected as a congresswoman from Montana.
After the election Mrs. O. G. Marksen was one of hundreds of women who wrote to her:
"We citizens . . . will back you up 100%.
You can depend on us—
can we depend on you?"

Chapter Eight
SIT DOWN, SISTER
1940–1968

———— ❧ ————

There had been a lot of changes in Congress.
There were more women—five in the House and two in the Senate.
The spittoons had been removed permanently, and a new ladies' restroom
had been built.

Jeannette worked for antiwar legislation.
Along with others in Congress, she denounced the Lend-Lease Act that
would allow American weapons to be sent overseas.
"Mothers alone can prevent our entering the war if they will express their
opinions now," she said.
In October 1940, President Roosevelt declared, "I've said this before, and I
shall say it again, and again, and again: Your boys are not going to be sent
to any foreign wars."
But that was before the surprise Japanese attack on American soil.

On December 7, 1941, Jeannette and her sister Edna
were at Jeannette's apartment in Washington, D.C.
They heard on the radio: "Pearl Harbor has been
attacked! The Japanese have bombed America!
WE ARE AT WAR!"

Most people thought that the only way to stop Hitler was to go to war.
Jeannette was about to take on the biggest challenge of her life—
but she knew what she had to do.
Unlike her vote in Congress against the Great War—now called
World War I—Jeannette did not have to talk to Wellington.
She did not need advice from friends and supporters.
She knew she had to take an immediate stand, even if it would be
for the last time.

When the war vote was read in the House, Jeannette stood up.
"Mr. Speaker, I object."
"You're out of order," he said.
"Mr. Speaker, I would like to be heard."
"Sit down, sister," he said.
"Mr. Speaker, point of order."
But Jeannette was ignored.

When Jeannette's name was called to cast her vote, she said,
"As a woman, I can't go to war, and I refuse to send anyone else."
Shouts and hisses rose from the floor of the House.
Not one other person voted "no."
Jeannette walked through a crush of people. Many grabbed her and
pushed her, demanding that she change her vote.
With her shoulders held back, Jeannette locked herself in the nearest
phone booth and called the Capitol police, asking them to escort her
safely to her office.

She made one phone call from her office that day.
"Wellington?" she said.
"Montana is one hundred and ten percent against you," he answered.
Later Jeannette told a friend, "I have nothing left except my integrity."

Letters from Montana flooded Jeannette's office.
"Oh, how ashamed I am to have to admit you are my
representative in Congress," said one writer.
The Cowpokes Union of Deer Lodge, Montana, wrote,
"In view of the bad storms in the offing [war],
the way you botched up the last branding [vote],
we would like to have you saddle up your bronco,
tie your bedroll on behind, and just ride home."
Newspapers called her vote a "swooning spell" and asked that she be
spanked with a hairbrush on the floor of the House.
One paper, the *Emporia Gazette* of Kansas, wrote something different.
"Probably one hundred men in Congress would have liked to do what she
did. None of them had the courage to do it. The *Gazette* entirely disagrees
with the wisdom of her position. But Lord, it was a brave thing!"

Jeannette knew her career in Congress was over.
After her term ended, she returned to Georgia, but she traveled to
Montana often to help care for her mother.
Jeannette kept reading and learning.
She studied the teachings of Mahatma Gandhi, who, instead of war,
practiced passive resistance to fight against British rule in India. She
traveled to India to see this for herself.
She wrote to a friend: "He [Gandhi] had two things he taught people:
truth and nonviolence. If his philosophy doesn't hold, we are lost."
Then she traveled across Africa, South America, Russia,
Turkey, and Indonesia—
listening to the people there, learning from them.

On a cold rainy day in
January 1968, Jeannette led
a march in Washington, D.C., to protest
the war in Vietnam.
Many Americans felt the reasons for the Vietnam War were
wrong, and they didn't want American soldiers fighting there.
Jeannette, too, was against the war, and against sending American boys
to fight on foreign soil. Five thousand women and children, called the
Jeannette Rankin Brigade, joined in her protest march to the Capitol.
"Wouldn't it be too bad if we left this world and hadn't done all we could for
peace?" Jeannette asked.
She was eighty-seven years old, and she was still fighting for what she believed in.